Who Reads?

Teacher's
Choice
Series

Betty Aynaga
Seaside, California

Illustrations by
Farmer Ted

Dominie Press, Inc.

The development of the *Teacher's Choice Series* was supported by the Reading Recovery project at California State University, San Bernardino. All authors' royalties from the sale of the *Teacher's Choice Series* will be used to support various Reading Recovery projects.

Publisher: Raymond Yuen
Series Editor: Stanley L. Swartz
Illustrator: Farmer Ted
Cover Designer: Steve Morris
Page Design: Pamela S. Pettigrew

Published by:

Dominie Press, Inc.
1949 Kellogg Avenue
Carlsbad, California 92008 USA

ISBN 1-56270-543-1

Printed in Singapore
9 10 11 12 13 VoZF 14 13 12 11 10

A cook reads.

A basketball player reads.

A doctor reads.

A farmer reads.

A rock star reads.

A president reads.

A teacher reads.

I read!

About the Author

Betty Aynaga has been a kindergarten and first grade teacher since 1982. She currently teaches a first grade bilingual class at Manzanita Elementary for the Monterey Peninsula Unified School District. Through literacy, her school aspires to create a "Better World for Every Child." Aside from her family and teaching, her loves are traveling, painting, walking along the beach, and of course, reading. She resides in Seaside, California with her husband and a cockatiel.